Crucibles

Published by
David J. Gingery Publishing LLC
P.O. Box 318
Rogersville, MO 65742

Web: http://www.gingerybooks.com
email: gingery@gingerybooks.com

Printed in the USA

Copyright © 2003 David J. Gingery Publishing LLC

All rights reserved

ISBN 1-878087-27-4

NOTICE OF DISCLAIMER: There are serious hazards in the processes and procedures in this book. No attempt has been made to point out all of the dangers or even a majority of them. The methods, materials and procedures that are suggested in this manual were developed by a non-professional. The author is not an engineer or scientist and no claim is made to the propriety of the methods suggested in these pages. The reader is fully responsible for devising safe procedures for every operation.

Both the author and David J. Gingery Publishing LLC hereby disclaim any liability for injury to persons or property that may result while using this book. Neither intends by this publication to explain all dangers known or unknown that may exist in the project described.

TABLE OF CONTENTS

Introduction 4
How crucibles were made 100 years ago. 6
Assembling the data 8
A PVC mold 11
Crucible composition. 20
A recipe for the clay mixture 23
Ramming up the crucible 26
Firing the crucible 29
Factors determining the life of a crucible 31
Making crucible tongs 34
Safety Precautions 36
Using the crucible for the first time 37
Making a concrete mold 39
Making the inner form for the concrete mold 44
The mold press 46
How to use the crucible machine 52
Top ten list of safety rules. 59
Final thoughts. 60
Typical sizes for clay/graphite crucibles. 60

Introduction...

When melting a substance, be it metal or mineral you need a container that has a higher melting point than the substance you're melting. Such containers are called crucibles. They can be made from a variety of materials, but those most commonly available commercially are made of clay, clay & graphite or silicon carbide.

Crucibles are sold by size, such as #6, #8 etc. The number of a crucible represents the approximate weight in pounds of aluminum that it will hold. So a #6 crucible will hold approximately six pounds of molten aluminum, a #8, eight pounds etc..

A crucible must be able to resist high temperatures without softening or becoming weak. It should not crack when exposed to sudden changes of temperature, as for instance when lifted out of a hot furnace and exposed to the air. It must be able to resist the corrosive action of fused substances, and of course it must not be porous.

The purpose of this booklet, is to help you decide whether or not it is practical to make clay crucibles in the home shop. No doubt, if you have been casting

Figure 1 #6 commercially made clay/graphite crucible.

metal for any length of time, the idea of purchasing or making a clay crucible has occurred to you. You may have got your start metal casting in the home shop with the charcoal furnace using a steel pot as a crucible. It might have been a plumbers lead pot, or you may have made a crucible by welding a disc to the end of a piece of pipe. Steel pots are functional, but there are contamination issues to consider when using them, particularly when melting brass. Therefore at some point you may decide they are no longer adequate for your needs and you begin considering the purchase of a commercially made crucible. You quickly discover that they are rather expensive and in some cases hard to find. Then, if you're like me, you start thinking; Geez, could I make one of these myself? Well, the answer is yes! But there are some important matters to consider.

First, making crucibles falls under the heading of pottery work. So as you contemplate making your own, it would be a good idea to get at least one good book on the subject of pottery making and read through it. One such book that I can recommend is, "The Complete Book Of Pottery Making" by John B. Kenny. I have an older edition of the book, but I ran a search and found it to still be in print and readily available.

Also, a word of caution before you begin. Acquire some experience melting and pouring metal before attempting to make and use your own clay crucibles. And keep in mind, all crucibles will fail. Yes, even the commercial ones. So always inspect your crucibles carefully before each use and handle them with care.

It is unlikely that you will be able to make a clay crucible on your own that is anywhere near the quality of a commercially made one. Many years of development have gone into the manufacture of commercial crucibles, and special formulas and techniques have been developed that we can not hope to duplicate in the home shop.

There is the advantage of a cost savings realized in making your own crucibles. But probably the main reason you are interested is to satisfy your own curiosity. It's that independent do-it-yourself attitude that many of us have. And that's an attitude to be proud of. Whether you realize it or not, when you make your own crucibles, you are preserving a lost technology. In essence, you are proving that yes, we can still make things on our own in this country. And if we have to, we can, as the old saying goes, "survive on a shoe string." Sadly, that trait seems to be lost in our affluent society. And history tells us that at some point we will be forced to survive on that shoe string again. And when that time comes, we will have proven we can do it.

How crucibles were made 100 years ago...

If you're still with me, you must have decided to at least be adventurous enough to investigate the idea of making your own crucibles further. If so, it would be advantageous to look at methods from long ago for ideas. So we begin with a look at three such methods as found in the 1899 work titled, "An Elementary Text-Book of Metallurgy" by A. Humbolt Sexton.

The Wheel Method: The clay is mixed with grog and rendered homogeneous by mixing or treading. The crucible maker sits before a rotating wheel on which is placed a core having the form of the interior of the crucible. He places a lump of clay over the core, and as the wheel is rotated, the clay is pressed down until the core is completely covered, and the exterior is roughly formed to the required shape. The exact form of the exterior and the thickness of the clay is then fixed by a gauge or template. The block is removed from the table and inverted, the finished crucible slips off, the spout is made with the fingers, and the crucible is dried and fired.

Casting Method: The clay is mixed as in method one. A flask, the interior of which has the shape of the exterior of the crucible is placed on a circular bottom in the center of which is a hole. The correct amount of clay is placed in the flask and a core the shape of the interior of the crucible is forced down into it. A central spike in the bottom of the core fits into the hole in the bottom of the flask and keeps the core central. The core is pressed into position, the clay rises between it and the flask and the crucible is made. See figure 3. The core is removed leaving the crucible with a hole in the bottom. The hole is stopped up with a small plug of clay and the crucible is then dried and fired.

Figure 2 *Illustrating the wheel method. From the book, "Pottery For Artists Craftsman & Teachers". Reprinted by Lindsay Publications.*

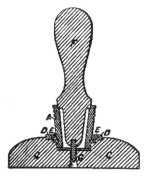

C, Base.
D, Brass ring.
A, Brass mould or flask.
F, Core.
G, Projecting point.

Figure 3 This is the set up for making a crucible as described in method 2. From the 1899 book, "An Elementary Text-Book of Metallurgy" by A. Humboldt Sexton.

Machine Method: A typical crucible machine for making clay/graphite crucibles in the early 20th century is shown in figure 4. It consisted of a rotating mold in which a weighed portion of clay and graphite are placed. Typically a good clay was mixed with 20 to 40 percent of its weight of graphite.

As the mold is rotated to make the clay fill the mold, an arm, or profile iron, assists the plastic material in assuming the

F, Flask.
M, Mandril.
C, Clay being formed into crucible.

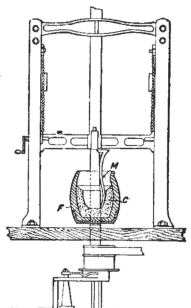

Figure 4 Typical crucible molding machine as it would have appeared in 1899. From the book, "An Elementary Text-Book of Metallurgy" by A. Humboldt Sexton.

proper shape and forms the walls at the correct thickness.

The crucible is then trimmed of all excess material at the top of the mold, and the latter is removed. After standing for 24 hours in a temperature of 70 to 80 degrees F., the crucible is smoothed up and then subjected for three weeks at a temperature sufficient to drive off all hygroscopic moisture. The remaining water is then driven off by placing the crucible for three days in the annealing oven in which a temperature of 1500 degrees is maintained.

After having been annealed or burned the crucible is placed in a loose-fitting clay mold termed a "seggar" or "sagger", to prevent excessive oxidation. It is kept for some time in a dry warm place, such as the top of an annealing oven. Crucibles are generally supposed to improve with age and are often kept for some time before being used.

Assembling the data. . .

As I reviewed the options, I decided not to attempt to make a crucible on a throw wheel as detailed in method one. For one thing, I didn't have a throw wheel. And since the method called for shaping the form by hand on a spinning wheel, I couldn't help but think the clay/grog mixture would have an abrasive effect. Kind of like holding my hands against a belt sander. Well, maybe not that bad.

The machine method for making a crucible detailed in #3, though interesting, seemed a bit too involved.

After giving the matter careful thought, I decided the method most applicable to the home shop would be similar to that in method two. I had also seen a similar idea presented in a 1938 Popular Science article by Leo G. Hall titled "Low-Cost crucibles." The process called for a mold with the inside diameter sized for the outer shape of the crucible and a core to fit inside that. With Hall's method, the clay mixture is inserted a little at a time into the top of the outer mold and rammed down thoroughly all around the inner mold. His mold looked very similar to that of our PVC mold in figure 5.

I was interested in developing a cheap, simple and easy

method of making molds. And finding a material to make the molds from was of primary concern. Certainly, molds made of steel or cast iron would be far superior, but large chunks of such material are expensive and difficult to acquire. I do have a metal lathe, but it isn't large enough to tackle the task of turning the inside bore in a mold for the size crucible I needed. So to clarify; What I was really looking for was something a bit more user friendly than a chunk of steel or cast iron to make molds from.

I began browsing the hardware store and local home improvement store for something that I could use for a mold that already had an inside bore close to the size of crucible I desired. I found what I was looking for in the plumbing isle, and that was 4" diameter PVC pipe and couplings. A cut away view of the PVC mold is shown in figure 5. The outer mold is made from two 4" PVC pipe couplings and short pieces of PVC pipe assembled with pipe cement. The taper on the inside wall of the mold was turned on the lathe.

The inner mold form is made of wood and also turned to size and taper on the lathe.

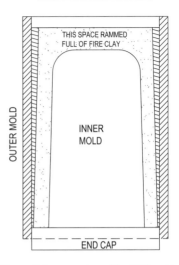

Figure 5 *Cutaway view of the PVC mold.*

To actually use the mold to make a crucible, the clay mixture is inserted into the top of the mold little by little and rammed down thoroughly all around the inner mold. When the mold is full, the compression plug is used in conjunction with a hammer and drill press to compact the clay further in the mold.

While the PVC mold was functional, I was limited as to the size of crucible I could make. I wanted to be able to make larger crucibles that duplicated the sizes and shapes of those available commercially.

So as I was working on the

PVC mold I kept considering the idea. As mentioned earlier, I wanted to avoid turning a large inside bore for the outer mold, so anything I came up with would have to take that into account.

Then it was suggested that a cheaper and more practical method of producing a crucible mold might be with concrete.

In simple terms, the idea was to turn two forms from wood representing the outside and the inside of the crucible on a mandrel between centers.

Then, make a box and position the outside wooden form in the center of the box. Smear grease on the form for a release agent and fill the box with concrete. When the concrete sets, remove the wooden form leaving a cavity representing the outside shape of the crucible.

Then complete the mold by suspending the inside wooden form inside the cavity that exists in the concrete mold.

To make a crucible, clay is rammed into the open space between the wall of the concrete mold and the inner form.

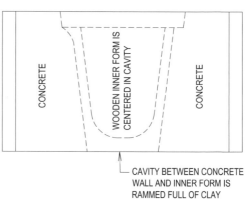

Figure 6 *A concrete mold for making crucibles.*

When the mold has been rammed full of clay, the finished crucible is pressed out, the inner form is removed and you have a finished crucible.

Figure 6 shows a basic representation of the idea. As you will see later in the book, I expand the idea further to include a press attachment that will aid in compacting the clay and removing the finished crucible from the mold.

Of the two methods detailed in this book, the concrete mold has produced the best crucibles. It also offers the advantage of being able to produce larger crucibles more closely representing those available commercially. But the PVC method has merit too so I'm going to present both methods beginning with the PVC method.

A PVC mold...

Though I was able to make satisfactory crucibles with the PVC method, the main drawback besides size limitations is that the inside taper can be no more than 2 degrees. At only 2 degrees, the finished crucible is a bit difficult to remove from the mold without damaging it.

For making larger crucibles, I urge you to consider the concrete mold method detailed later in the book because it is far superior to the PVC method detailed here. Also, if you want to make smaller #1 or #2 crucibles consider substituting the PVC pipe used for the outer mold for a block of steel or aluminum. It would be more

Figure 7 *The components for the outer mold. Two 4" PVC couplings are shown in the background. Two 1-5/8" long pieces of 4" PVC pipe are in the foreground along with one 3-1/2" long piece of PVC pipe.*

Figure 9 *Apply glue to the other end of the pipe and inside coupling and assemble as shown.*

Figure 10 *Apply glue to each of the 1-5/8" long end pieces and insert one into each end of the coupling. Press the end pieces in until they are flush against the inside center stop band of the coupling. This will leave a 3/8" deep ledge on both ends of the coupling.*

Figure 8 *Apply PVC glue to one end of the 3-1/2" long piece of PVC pipe and the inside of one end of a coupling. Insert the pipe into the coupling all the way to the center band.*

work to bore out a block of steel or aluminum, but for making smaller crucibles it would be practical.

To make a PVC mold, you will need two 4" PVC couplings, two pieces of 4" PVC pipe 1-5/8" long and one piece of 4" PVC pipe 3-1/2" long as shown in figure 7. Assemble the individual pieces with PVC glue as shown in figures 8, 9 and 10.

After assembly, you will notice a gap between sections as noted in figure 11. The gap can be filled with an epoxy putty such as shown in figure 12 or with auto body putty. Simply follow the mixing instructions on the package or can and then press the putty firmly into the gap.

When the putty has hardened, mount the PVC form in the lathe to turn the inside taper. I was able to hold the form with

Figure 11 *When assembled there will be a gap between the sections of pipe. The gap can be filled with epoxy such as that shown in figure 12.*

Figure 13 *The set up for boring the inside taper in the outer mold.*

a four jaw chuck adjusted to grip from the inside. Center the work in the chuck, mount a boring bar and adjust the compound rest to turn the 2 degree taper. The travel of the compound rest will not be sufficient to finish the entire length of the taper so you will have to do it in sections. As each section is completed,

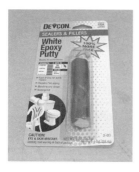

Figure 12 *Epoxy such as shown in the photo can be used to fill in the gap in the inside mold. This product or one similar can be found at just about any hardware store or home center.*

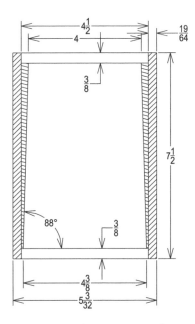

Figure 14 Sectioned view of the outer mold.

Figure 15 Applying polyurethane to the inside surface of the mold.

move the carriage forward, lock it in position, readjust the boring bar and finish that section. A good sharp cutter and a fairly fast feed are needed to prevent the plastic from softening due to overheating. Any gouges or imperfections can be filled later with epoxy and sanded smooth.

After the taper is turned, sand the inside surface smooth. Fill any gouges with epoxy and re-sand. Then coat the inside wall of the mold with gloss polyurethane. Three coats are sufficient, and it is best to sand between each coat for a smoother surface.

The inner form for the PVC mold is made from a block of wood measuring 6-1/2" long x 3-1/2" square. Such a block of wood can be made by gluing together two 2 x 4 boards and one 1 x 4 board each slightly longer than 6-1/2". When the glue has dried, ensure that both ends of the block are square. Then find and mark the center

Figure 16 Inner mold form.

13

location in one end of the block as shown in figure 16. A lathe will be needed to turn the outside form. If turning the block on a metal lathe, you can make a mandrel for the job that can be mounted in a 3-jaw chuck. The drawings show the detail for the mandrel assembly.

The mandrel collar is shown in figure 17 and is made from a 5/8" length of 1-1/2" diameter c.r.s. round with the inside diameter bored to 1". A hole is drilled in the side and tapped for a 1/4-20 set screw.

The mandrel flange shown in figure 18 is made from a large flat washer or machinery bushing.

Assemble the flange and collar as shown in figure 19 and secure by brazing the joint.

The mandrel shaft is a 2-1/2" length of c.r.s. round as shown in figure 20.

The mandrel center shown in figure 21 is made from a 3/4" length of 1/4-20 threaded rod.

The exploded view of the assembly being mounted to the inner mold form is shown in figure 22. The mandrel center threads into the end of the mandrel and is aligned with the center mark in the end of the mold blank. A rap with the hammer drives the point into the block. The indention left in the end of the block by the center point will serve as an

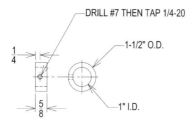

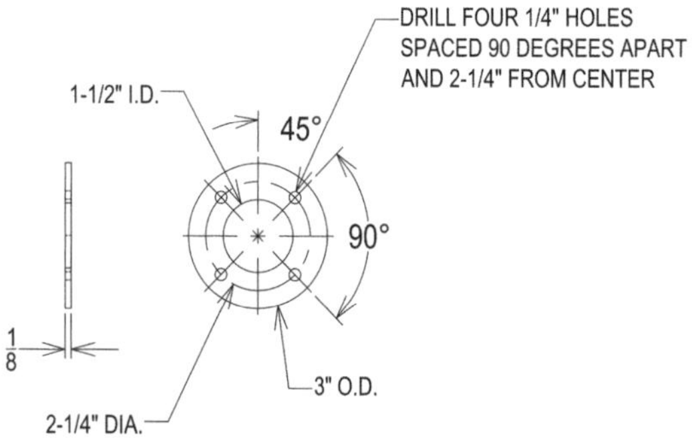

Figure 17 Mandrel collar. Make one from 1-1/2" diameter c.r.s. round.

Figure 18 Mandrel flange. Make one from a 1" flat washer.

BRAZE THE JOINT TO SECURE THE FLANGE TO THE COLLAR.

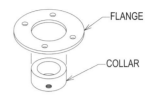
FLANGE
COLLAR

Figure 19 The flange/collar assembly.

important reference later. As you can see in the drawing, figure 22, the flange/collar is bolted to the end of the block with 1/4" x 1-1/2" lag screws and the mandrel is secured with a set screw.

The mandrel is mounted in the 3-jaw chuck on the lathe. The end of the blank is center drilled to support it between centers as shown in figure 24.

The rough form or diameter of the blank is turned using a round nose wood lathe tool. If you are using a metal lathe, a boring bar can serve as a tool rest as shown in figure 24 and 25.

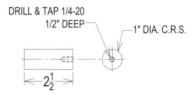

Figure 20 The mandrel shaft. Make one from 1" diameter c.r.s. round.

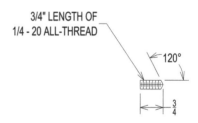

Figure 21 Mandrel center. Make 1 from 1/4-20 threaded rod.

15

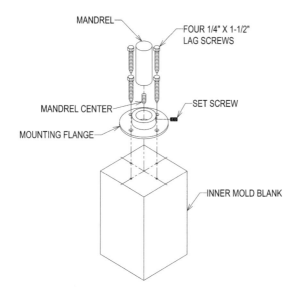

Figure 22 Exploded view of mandrel assembly being attached to the inner mold blank. The photo at left shows the mandrel mounted to the mold blank.

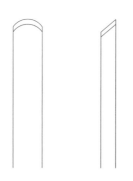

Figure 23 Round nose lathe tool detail.

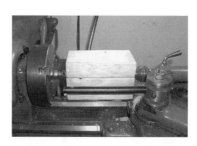

Figure 24 The inner mold form as it appears set up between centers in the metal lathe. Note the boring bar positioned to serve as a tool rest.

The proper way to apply the round nose tool to the work is to hold it level, and perfectly flat on the tool rest. The gap between the tool rest and the work should be approximately 1/16". As the work is turned down, you will need to advance the tool rest to keep the gap within that range.

To finish the diameter of the form and turn the taper, remove the tail stock center and set the compound rest at two degrees. Keep in mind that the boring bar

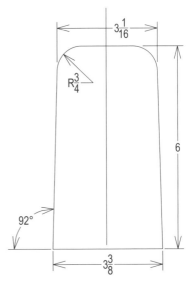

Figure 27 Inner mold detail.

Figure 25 Using a 1/2" round nose lathe tool to rough the outside form of the inner mold.

will have to be long enough to travel the length of the work, in this instance 7" long. Since the travel of the compound rest is not sufficient to do the work in a single pass, it will be necessary

Figure 26 Turning the outside taper of the form using the boring bar.

Figure 28 Checking the end diameter of the inner form with calipers.

17

Figure 29 Forming the end radius with a surform® or wood forming tool.

to do the work in sections, advancing the saddle forward as needed to cut the full length of the form.

Finished dimensions for the inner form are shown in figure 27.

The radius on the end of the mold can be formed with a surform® or wood forming tool as shown in figure 29.

Figure 30 Sanding the surface of the inner mold with 100 grit paper..

Sand the surface of the wooden form with 100 grit paper. Fill gouges and imperfections with wood putty or auto body putty and resand to a smooth surface.

Remove the finished inner mold from the lathe. Remove the mandrel from the flange/collar and secure it in the 3-jaw chuck with the 1/4-20 threaded hole facing out.

Now make the inner mold end cap. Start by drilling a 1/4" hole in the center of a 4-3/4" diameter wooden disk. Mount

Figure 31 Turning the radius of the inner mold end cap.

the wooden disk on the end of the mandrel using a 1/4-20 bolt and flat washer. Reduce the diameter of the disk to 4-1/2" or until it will just fit in the end of the outer mold.

Remove the end cap from the lathe and counter bore the center hole to 1" diameter, 1/4"

Figure 32 Counter bore the center hole of the inner mold end cap to 1" diameter, 1/4" deep.

of the outer mold which in this instance is 4". When finished, fill the center hole with wood putty or auto body putty. Sand the surface smooth and apply three coats of polyurethane.

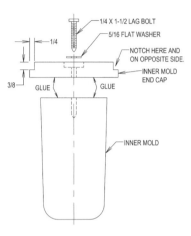

Figure 33 The inner mold assembly.

deep as shown in figure 32. Cut a notch on opposite sides of the end cap as detailed in figure 33. The purpose of the notches will become evident later when it becomes necessary to grip the inner mold in the vise.

Apply wood glue to the bottom of the inner cap and the top of the inner mold. Center the end cap on the end of the mold and secure with a 1/4" x 1-1/2" lag bolt as shown by the drawing in figure 33. After the glue sets, apply three coats of polyurethane, sanding between coats to achieve a smooth finished surface. A photo of the completed inner mold is shown in figure 34.

The compression plug is made in the same manner as the end cap, except its diameter is turned to fit the inside diameter

Figure 34 The completed inner mold. Notice the notch on the opposite sides of the end cap. The purpose of the notches will be evident when it becomes necessary to separate the inner mold from the clay crucible.

Figure 35 *The completed PVC mold. Compression plug on left. The outer mold at center, and the inner mold on the right.*

Crucible composition...

The primary ingredient in crucibles is *clay*. Clay can best be described as those types of earth that become plastic when wet and harden when heated. The *plastic or plasticity* of clay refers to its workability. Or in other words its ability to change form under pressure and to maintain that form after the pressure is removed.

Clays are composed chiefly of aluminum silicates mixed with other minerals and they will vary in color depending on their content. For instance, clays with 1% of iron will fire red and titanium increases this color. Yellow clays contain iron as a free hydrate. All clays contain quartz sand and sometimes mica. *Fireclay*, the clay we are most concerned with, is a clay composed mainly of silicate of aluminum and is capable of withstanding very high temperatures.

Though clay is a primary ingredient of the crucibles, clay by itself contracts very much on heating. To reduce the shrink effect and to strengthen the crucible, a refractory substance must be mixed in with the clay. Substances often used are as follows...

Grog: A clay that has been fired and then crushed and ground up into small particles. Crucibles made of clay and grog, though very functional, require a high degree a care when in use. Their life expectancy is not anywhere near as long as a clay/graphite crucible. Clay crucibles will absorb moisture from the air over time, so before each use they must be preheated to a temperature above the boiling point of water to drive out any moisture they may contain.

***Graphite*:** Also called Plumbago is a natural variety of elemental carbon having a grayish black color and a metallic tinge. It occurs in two forms: foliated and amorphous. Foliated (crystalline graphite) is used primarily for crucibles and lubricants. Amorphous graphite (uncrystallized) is used primarily for lead pencils, foundry facings, electric brush carbons and paint pigment.

Crucibles which contain graphite are called Plumbago crucibles. The graphite content of such crucibles is normally in the range of 30-40% of the total weight of the crucible.

Plumbago (clay graphite) crucibles are in wide use today and are superior to crucibles that contain only clay and grog. They are very refractory, will support sudden changes of temperature without cracking, do not become weak at high temperatures, are very smooth so that shots of metal do not adhere to them, and they can be used over and over again.

The major challenge in making clay/graphite crucibles is that they must be formed under high pressure and annealed for three days at 1500 degrees before use. See method 3 on pages 7 & 8 for a review of the information on making clay graphite crucibles.

Silicon/Carbide: A bluish-black crystalline artificial mineral (SiC) containing silica and carbon. Used in a refractory material it is bonded with clays or held together with its own crystals by a method of recrystallization. Silicon carbide is made by fusing sand and coke with sawdust, using salt as a flux. Temperatures required for the process are in the range of 4000 degrees F..

The process was developed in 1891 by E.G. Acheson. Pure silicon carbide will contain 70% silicon and 30% of carbon. Crucibles containing silicon carbide are far superior to clay/grog or clay/graphite crucibles and silicon carbide crucibles do not have to be annealed before use.

21

Other ingredients that might be added to crucible formulas are *Potash Feldspar:* (Orthoclase). (K2OAl2O3-6SiO2), a vitreous substance containing potassium and aluminum silicate. When added in small amounts to the clay mix (usually 2% or less) it acts as flux helping the clay body to fuse better in firing. But too much Feldspar will reduce the refractoriness of the clay and tend to make it less plastic.

Also, various clay types and mixtures of clays may be used in order to change the plasticity and improve the workability of a mixture. For instance if you were making a crucible on a wheel as in method one, you would want the clay mixture to be more plastic. So you would likely choose a finer clay such as one of the Ball clays. And in some instances it might be desirable to add Kaolin (pure clay) to a mixture to enhance the plasticity of a clay body even further.

A recipe for the clay mixture. . .

I came across several recipes for making crucibles, some of which were fairly complex. After some experimentation, the following recipe seemed to work as well as any I tried. It will require approximately 3 pounds to fill the PVC mold so this recipe is for a 3 pound mix.

Hawthorne bond 35 fire clay 38%, or 18 ounces. (Or other fire clay may be substituted.)

Potash Feldspar 2%, or 3/4 ounce.

Brick grog 20 mesh 60%, or 29 ounces.

All of the ingredients above, including fire clay can be purchased at any good pottery supply house. We are often asked where fire clay can be purchased. The best place to look is in the yellow pages under pottery supplies. If not there, run an internet search by typing pottery supplies or pottery clay in the search line and you will find numerous suppliers many of whom will be glad to provide mail order service.

In addition to the ingredients in the recipe, you will need a large plastic container with lid, a measuring cup, a small scale and a spatula or wooden stick for mixing.

The set of photos in figures 36 through 43 will take you through the process of mixing up a batch of clay for a crucible.

A side note. . .

I had some commercial castable refractory left over when I built my furnace. Just out of curiosity I took the left over refractory and made a couple of crucibles. I just added a bit of water to the dry mix until it was just damp, and then rammed it in the mold just as I did with the clay recipe. They turned out to be satisfactory crucibles and I was able to get several pours from them.

F.Y.I. Castable refractory is a commercial product used to form the walls in furnaces. It is also used for flues, combustion chambers etc. It is a blend of clay, aggregate, grog and other ingredients. I purchased mine in 50 pound bags from McMaster Carr.

www.mcmastercarr.com

Also available from. . .
www.budgetcastingsupply.com

Figure 36 Begin by adding the grog to the bowl. In this instance, the end mixture needs to render 3 pounds dry weight so to make the math easier, convert the 3 pounds to 48 oz.. The grog requirement is 60% of the mixture so (.60 x 48) equals 28.8 oz. which can be rounded up to <u>29 oz.</u>.

Figure 37 Now add 2% by weight of Potash Feldspar. (.02 x 48 oz.) = .96 oz. which I rounded down to <u>3/4 oz.</u>.

Figure 38 Mix the two ingredients together thoroughly.

Figure 39 Now add 38% by weight of clay. (.38 x 48) = 18.24 ounces. I rounded this number up to 19 ounces.

Figure 40 Mix the dry ingredients together thoroughly.

Figure 41 Gradually moisten the mixture with water. It won't take much, probably less than 1 cup. You can use your hands to do the mixing. You're looking for a slightly damp crumbly mixture kind of like home made bread crumbs. See next figure.

Figure 42 Here you see how the completed mixture looks in my hand. It feels slightly damp, but not wet and has a crumbly texture. You don't want to over water the mixture, because if it's too wet, it will stick to the sides of the mold making the crucible impossible to remove without causing damage. Too dry and the mixture won't bind together. With a little trial & error, you will get it just right.

Figure 43 Cover the mixture and let it cure overnight.

25

Ramming up a crucible...

When you're ready to ram up a crucible, the following photos and descriptions will guide you through the process.

Figure 44 Assembled PVC mold. Coat the inside surfaces of the mold with a light layer of petroleum jelly. This works as a release agent, making the finished crucible easier to remove from the mold.

Figure 45 Ram the clay into the mold. A 3/8" x 3/4" pine stick about 18" long works very well for this purpose. Don't try to cram in all the clay at once, but rather work it in layers. Add a little clay and then ram in all around, then another layer and so on. You want the crucible rammed firmly and evenly all the way through. Loose areas will cause weak spots in finished product. Fill the mold 1/8" or so above the inside lip.

Figure 46 The clay must be compressed very tight. Use the drill press in conjunction with the compression disk to compress the clay further.

Figure 47 The clay form is ready to be removed from the mold.

Figure 48 You must loosen the inner mold first and a strap wrench will work well for this purpose. Such a wrench can be purchased at most hardware or discount stores.

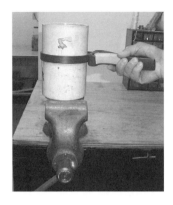

Figure 49 Secure the inner mold form end cap in the vise. Now you know what the notches in the end cap were for. Grip the outer mold form with the strap wrench and begin applying force to loosen the clay form from the inner mold. When you can easily twist the outer mold around by hand you are ready to press the crucible from the outer mold. Ensure that the inner form remains in position for the next step.

Figure 50 The drill press works well for forcing the crucible from the mold too. As mentioned in the last step, ensure that the inner mold is still in position to support the form. Position the edges of the outer mold on spacer strips as shown in the photo. The spacer strips should be thick enough to allow 1/2" or so of space for the crucible to drop. Finally, position the compression disk on crucible and apply pressure with the drill press until the crucible separates from the mold.

Figure 51 Carefully transport the mold to the work bench, then raise the outer mold to reveal the crucible.

Figure 52 Carefully turn the finished crucible over to remove the outer form.

Figure 53 The spout on the edge of the lip was formed by applying a lump of clay to the side of the crucible body and shaping it by hand. For this process, the inner form must be in place to support the wall. After the spout has been formed, remove the inner form and cut a small notch in the inside lip with a utility knife.

Firing the crucible. . .

Before the crucible can be put to use, it must be fired. The purpose of firing is to drive out all moisture and harden or mature the clay. But before firing, the crucible must be bone dry. That condition is achieved by first allowing it to air dry for a few days. Then it is placed in an oven and baked at a temperature of 250 degrees for a couple of hours to drive out

Figure 54 A crucible after firing.

the remaining residual moisture. The kitchen oven works well for this. While the crucible is still hot from the oven it is put directly in the furnace or kiln and gradually heated over a period of 3 to 4 hours to a temperature of approximately 2000 degrees.

Many methods for firing pottery can be employed. From an open pit in the ground fired by wood to a state of the art electric or gas fired kiln. Chances are if you are interested in making crucibles you already have a furnace of some type. If you can melt metal in the furnace, you can fire a clay crucible in it.

As mentioned, the crucible will have to be fired to a temperature of at least 2000 degrees. It is not likely you will have a pyrometer but you can judge temperature by color and achieve acceptable results. The color chart in figure 56 compares temperature with color.

I fire my crucibles in an electric kiln and use what are called *pyrometric cones* to determine when the desired temperature has been achieved.

If you have done reading on ceramics or pottery you will likely be familiar with *Pyrometric cones*. They are small

Figure 55 *Before firing your crucible, examine it carefully to ensure it is free from defect. The photo above pictures a crucible that has not been rammed tight enough. You can tell by the layering effect of the clay. Such a crucible should not be used.*

pyramids of clay with fluxes added to cause them to melt at known temperatures. Pyrometric cones are numbered 022 through 42 with each number representing a different temperature. A cone that corresponds with the temperature you want to achieve is placed on a corresponding stand in the kiln along with the items being fired. It is positioned so that it will be in plain view when looking through a peep hole in the side of the kiln. I use the #03 cone which corresponds with 2000 degrees F. When it is determined that the kiln is getting near the desired temperature, I begin checking the cone periodically by looking through the peephole. When the desired temperature has been reached the cone will bend and when that happens I know that it is time to shut off the kiln.

Do not remove the crucibles from the kiln until they have cooled completely. Removing a crucible before it is cooled completely could cause damage such as a cracked or otherwise weakened crucible.

COLOR	DEGREES F.
Lowest visible red to cherry red	885 to 1200
Dark red to cherry red	1200 to 1380
Cherry red to bright cherry red	1380 to 1500
Bright cherry red to orange	1500 to 1650
Orange to yellow	1650 to 2000
Yellow to light yellow	2000 to 2400

Figure 56 Color scale for temperatures.

Factors determining the life of a crucible...

Commercial clay/graphite crucibles that have been thoroughly dried will seldom spall or crack when heated. The fine cracks that occasionally develop after they have been in service for some time are usually due to hot gases and improper annealing. When a crucible cracks and the contents run out, the crucible is said to run.

Our clay/grog crucibles will not be as reliable as commercial crucibles. They will be much more susceptible to cracking so you will have to check them carefully before each pour.

Although clay crucibles are free from moisture when removed from the kiln, they rapidly absorb it again from the surrounding air. A damp crucible put directly into a hot furnace, or into a cold one and heated too rapidly, could cause trapped moisture to change to steam. And the steam created, could blow pieces of the crucible off. For this reason clay crucibles, even commercial clay/graphite crucibles must be annealed before each use. This is done by raising them from room temperature to a temperature somewhat above the boiling point of water so that any moisture they contain may be slowly driven off.

An oxidizing atmosphere (too rich in oxygen) will damage a crucible and weaken it, and if an oxidizing flame is trained directly on a crucible, the crucible will become badly scored at that point. So for longer crucible life in any furnace, especially in oil or gas furnaces, the optimum flame will be neutral or slightly carburizing, which means just a tiny bit short of oxygen.

Not removing the pot from the furnace when the metal is ready to pour, or allowing the metal to soak, increases the wear on the crucible. So promptness in pouring will lengthen the life of any crucible. Also, the higher the temperature of a metal is raised, the more wear on the crucible.

Another way in which crucibles are damaged is by wedging them full of cold ingots or scrap. The problem with this is that the cold metal will expand when heated to the melting point. The crucible does not expand very much, so a great strain is put on the walls of a crucible. This could cause the crucible to crack or at the very least be weakened.

Crucibles may also be damaged by carelessness in poking the fire or in knocking off slag or clinkers.

The life of a crucible will be extended if you keep it hot continuously and don't allow it to cool. That's because heating and cooling causes expansion and contraction which places a strain on the crucible. This is particularly true with our clay/grog crucibles. If you are unable to keep the crucible hot, you can minimize the damage caused by expansion and contraction by placing the empty crucible back in the furnace immediately after pouring so that it can cool gradually with the furnace.

Another way to extend the life of a crucible is to apply a protective coating or glaze to its inside and outside surface after it has been fired. But do not apply glaze to the bottom exterior of the crucible. I learned this the hard way when the glaze on the bottom of my crucible caused it to bond to the plinth of my furnace.

Commercial glazes are made, but may be hard to find. You can make your own glaze mix from ground glass, clay and borax.

Begin by pulverizing two or three glass bottles to the point of reducing them to sand again. Be certain to wear eye protection when you pulverize bottles.

You can put the bottles in a sack and break them into small pieces first. Then stand a 16" length of 1-1/4" pipe on a cake of iron or steel about 1/2" thick and drop a few pieces of glass in the pipe. Pound the glass with a length of 3/4" steel rod about 2' long to pulverize it. The improvised mortar and pestle described above reduces the danger, but occasional chips of glass will fly about so you must be careful for yourself and bystanders. Sift the glass through a small tea strainer and return all that won't pass to the piece of pipe for another pounding.

Add to the ground glass one half its volume of fire clay and one fourth its volume of borax powder. Mix the dry ingredients thoroughly. Then add water and mix to the consistency of thinned paint. (Like rich cream) Mix only enough for each use.

To apply the glaze, first wet the surface of the crucible by brushing on water. Then apply a uniform coat of glaze with a brush. You must stir often and add water from time to time for it tends to settle and thicken as you work. Once the surface is coated, refire the crucible to at least 2000 degrees to fuse the lining. The result is a hard and durable surface that resists moisture absorption.

Making Crucible tongs...

It is not difficult to make a set of crucible tongs, but care must be taken to make them fit properly.

3/16" x 3/4" hot rolled steel is adequate for crucibles up to a #6, but 1/4" x 3/4" stock should be used for a #8 crucible. Metal of this weight can be cold forged, but it will require less force if you heat it to a bright red heat.

Begin with two bars of 3/16" x 3/4" hot rolled steel 36" long. Drill a 5/16" hole 7" from the end of each bar. Join the two bars together with a 5/16" rivet.

Heat the area below the pivot to a bright red heat and clamp it in the vise about one inch below the pivot and give it

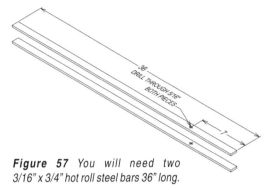

Figure 57 You will need two 3/16" x 3/4" hot roll steel bars 36" long.

Figure 59 Join both bars together with a 5/16" rivet. (A bolt & nut will not be reliable)

Figure 58 Drill a 5/16" hole centered 7" from the end of both bars.

a half twist with a wrench as shown in figure 61. This work must be done quickly before the metal cools so have the vise and wrench adjusted and ready before you heat the metal.

Now you have what might be used as a simple forge tongs as shown in figure 62. The gripping members can be shaped to many special purposes. One

Figure 60 Heat the area below the pivot to a bright red heat.

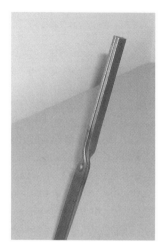

Figure 62 Forge tongs

Figure 61 Clamp the tongs in a vise about 1" below the pivot and give it a half twist with a wrench.

practical use for such tongs is to add metal to a partly full crucible of molten metal. (Never drop it in).

The next step is to shape the gripping members to fit the crucible. Begin by bending them out sharply and then forge them to fit the curve of the crucible. You can use scraps of large pipe or metal disks that are near the size of the crucible as a form. See figure 63. Then final adjustments can be made to fit the tongs to the contour of the crucible.

It will improve the tongs to bend an angle of one or two degrees near the pivot to reduce stooping during the pouring.

Figure 63 Shaping to fit the crucible.

Safety precautions . . .

These precautions have been mentioned before in our other publications. But it is worthwhile to consider them again because safety should be foremost in your mind at all times.

First of all, it is extremely dangerous to spill molten metal on any damp surface especially concrete or stone. Molten metal if dropped on such surfaces, will explode and shower the area with molten metal and bits of hot rock. It's best to prepare a sand bed about 2" thick and at least 3 or 4 feet square for your pour area and then don't carry a pot of metal outside that bed area.

Never allow metal to solidify in the pot. As a precaution, provide a place to get rid of all that you plan to melt. A muffin tin such as that in figure 69 works well for aluminum and pot metal. A series of dents could also be pressed into the bed of sand to form small ingot molds.

Wear glasses when you look into the vent hole of the furnace. Don't wear highly flammable clothing. You are certain to step on hot metal or spill a dab, and your feet are in great danger. So wear good leather shoes. No sneakers or sandals!

Make tongs to fit each size crucible you use and never handle a crucible with improperly fitting tongs. Before moving the crucible from the furnace, make sure you have an absolutely firm grip. Clear the area of anything that might trip you up as you carry the pot to the mold, and never walk backwards. Plan your work so you can move forward in a circle to pour your molds and return the empty pot safely to the furnace immediately after the pour.

It is a certain fact that all crucibles will fail at some point. (Yes even the commercial ones) So careful inspection is re-

Figure 64 *An example of a damaged crucible. The cracks are obvious and extend through the wall of the crucible.* ***Never use a damaged crucible!***

quired before each melt. Never attempt to melt anything in a cracked or damaged crucible. A crucible that breaks during a pour is a frightening thing. And if the molten metal were to splash on clothing or body parts it could be disastrous. I don't want to scare you to death, but you need to be cautious and aware of the danger. The risk is always there, but if you use common sense, the risks can be managed. If you are new to metal casting, you should gain experience in the foundry before making and using your own crucibles. Pouring metal requires extreme caution and every move must be carefully planned. With experience you will develope a familiarity with the process which will enable you to look ahead, anticipate problems before they happen and know how to react accordingly.

Using the crucible for the first time. . .

Clay crucibles will absorb moisture from the air even over a short period of time. So each time you use a clay crucible, it will need to be preheated to a temperature of 250 degrees for an hour or so to drive out any residual moisture. I do this in the kitchen oven, then transfer the crucible from the kitchen oven directly to the melting furnace. The crucible should be preheated empty so don't add any metal to it until the furnace reaches melting temperature.*

Just before pouring, skim the impurities (dross) from the surface of the melt and discard.

Carefully grasp the crucible with the tongs, remove it from the furnace, and carry it to the mold and begin the pour. When the pour is complete empty the remaining molten metal. A discarded muffin tin works well for this. Never allow molten metal to solidify in the crucible. Put the empty crucible back in the furnace immediately. Close the furnace and allow the crucible to cool slowly along with the furnace. Rapid heating and cooling can really damage clay crucibles.

*Before using the crucible for the first time, review the top ten list on page 60.

Figure 65 Skimming the dross from the top of the melt.

Figure 66 Removing the crucible from the furnace.

Figure 67 Transporting the crucible to the mold.

Figure 68 Pouring aluminum into the mold.

Figure 69 Emptying the excess aluminum into a muffin tin. The ingots created by the cup mold are just the right size for the foundry.

Making a concrete mold...

A cheap and easy crucible mold can be made with concrete.

You begin by assembling and turning the form representing outside shape of the crucible.

The blank form consists of stacked, predrilled octagons of wood assembled with glue and drawn snug over the mandrel with nuts and washers. See figure 71. The mandrel can be a length of 3/4" diameter threaded rod. Please note that if the individual pieces of wood are warped in any way it may be necessary to further clamp them together at the edges with bar clamps.

Figure 71 Elements of the stacked form. Here we are applying glue to the each octagon of wood.

Figure 72 The outer form mounted between centers on the lathe.

After the glue dries, the form is turned in the lathe on a mandrel between centers to the dimensions shown in figure 70.

To complete the outer form, you will need to fashion the pouring spout at the top edge with auto body putty or epoxy putty. The outer form with spout is shown in figure 73.

The complete outer form assembly consists of the end cap, the bottom board and the

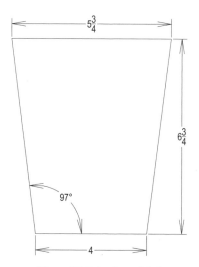

Figure 70 Outer form detail.

39

Figure 73 The completed outer form. The spout can be formed on the top edge of the form as shown with auto body putty or epoxy putty.

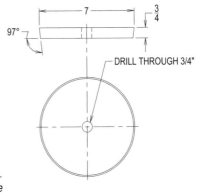

Figure 74 The end cap.

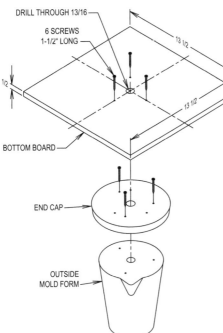

Figure 75 The expanded view of the complete outer form assembly. When assembled, fill all imperfections with putty, sand smooth and apply three coats of polyurethane. The finished form should look like the photo on the right.

outer form. The end cap shown in figure 74, is a wooden disk turned to a 7" diameter with a 7 degree taper. The bottom board is a 13-1/2" square piece of 1/2" plywood. Assemble the above mentioned pieces as shown in figure 75, then finish with three coats of polyurethane

The mold box detail is shown in figure 76. The sides consist of 3/4" exterior grade plywood with inside dimensions measuring 12" x 12". The depth of the box is to be 3/4" deeper than the combined height of the outer form and end cap. In this instance 7-1/2" deep. The sides are assembled with deck screws or nails using 1-1/2" x 1-1/2" wooden cleats in each corner. Also note the four 1/2" x 3" threaded bolts. Two of each are installed in the two opposite sides of the box, the purpose of which is to attach 2 x 4 support posts as shown in the figure 76. As you will see later, the posts are used to aid in the removal of the mold form after the concrete sets.

Coat the outer form in figure 75 with a release agent. A thin coating of oil or petroleum jelly will do fine. But before applying the release agent, apply a piece of duct tape over the 3/4" through hole as shown in figure 78.

Now insert the form into the mold box and Secure the plywood base to the edges of the box with 1-1/2" long #8 wood

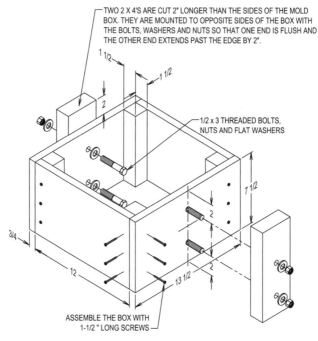

Figure 76 Concrete mold box detail.

41

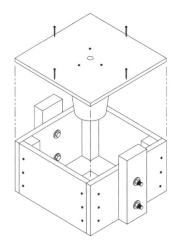

Figure 77 Installing the outer form assembly in the concrete mold box.

Figure 78 The assembled mold. Note the piece of duct tape over the center through hole.

screws as shown in figure 77.

Turn the box over and ensure the piece of duct tape covers the hole in the form.

We are now ready to fill the box with concrete. It will require approximately 5/8 of a cubic foot of concrete to fill the mold. An 80# bag of ready to use concrete mix such as Quikrete® will do the job with a little left over. Mix according to the instructions on the bag and tamp the concrete into the mold box paying particular attention to work it well into the corners and around the inner form. When the mold is full, rap the sides of the box several times with a rubber mallet to force any trapped air to the surface. Then strike the mold off level and wait for at least 2 days for the concrete to cure.

After the concrete has cured we are ready to remove the wooden form from the mold.

The drawing in figure 80 shows the steps for removing the wooden form from the concrete mold.

A 2 x 4 with a 3/4" hole drilled through the center is laid across both side posts. A length of threaded rod is inserted through the cross board and the wooden form so that it extends out the back of the mold. Nuts and lock washers are threaded on each end. Tightening the nut as shown will draw the wooden form from the mold revealing the outer shape of the crucible in the concrete.

There will likely be a few

Figure 79 Here we see the concrete has cured, the tape has been removed and the wooden form is ready to be removed from the mold.

small air holes left in the concrete and these can be filled with auto body putty. Sand smooth and when the concrete is thoroughly dry, apply three coats of polyurethane to the inside wall of the mold to seal it and give a nice smooth finish. Sand as necessary between coats.

The finished concrete portion of your mold will look like that in figure 81.

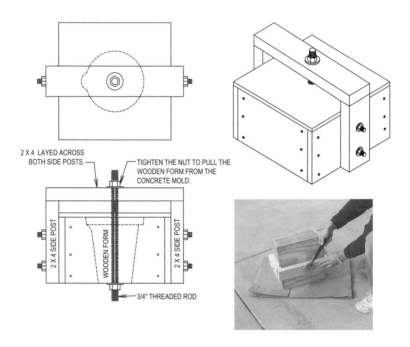

Figure 80 Removing the wooden form from the concrete mold. A 2 x 4 with a 3/4" hole in the center is laid across both legs. A length of threaded rod is inserted as shown and as the nuts are tightened, the wooden form is pulled from the mold.

43

Figure 81 The concrete mold. The wooden form has been removed. Air holes in the cavity wall have been filled and sanded and three coats of polyurethane have been applied to the inside surface.

Making the inner form...

The inner form for the crucible mold is made in the same manner as the outer form for the concrete mold. That is, glue together wooden blocks to form the blank and then turn the form between centers to dimensions shown in figure 82.

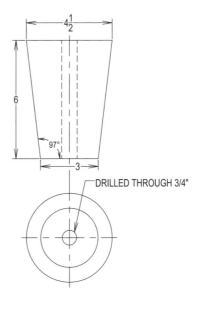

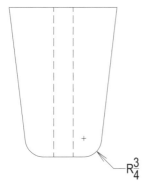

Figure 82 The wooden blank for the inner form is assembled from wooden disks just like we did earlier. Then the form is mounted on a threaded rod in the lathe and turned between centers to the size and taper shown above.

The complete inner form assembly is shown in figure 83 and consists of three pieces. The end cap which is made exactly like that in figure 74 on page 40, a 20" long 2 x 4 board with a 3/4" hole drilled through the center, and the inner form. The items mentioned above are assembled on a 3/4" wooden dowel 8" long and are held together with wood screws and wood glue.

Apply wood glue as shown to the top of the inner mold, both surfaces of the end cap and the corresponding area on the bottom side of the 2 x 4. Glue is also applied to the wooden dowel which is then inserted

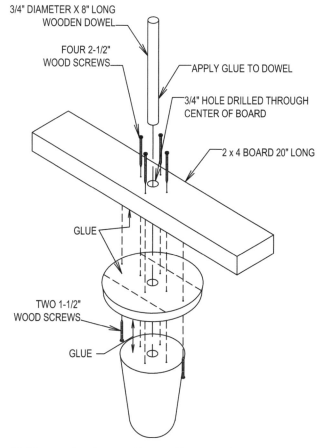

Figure 83 *The complete inner mold assembly. Apply glue where shown and assemble with screws and wooden dowel.*

through 3/4" holes in all three pieces. The pieces are further secured with wood screws as shown in the drawing.

When the glue has dried, fill uneven areas and holes with putty. Sand smooth and finish with 3 coats of polyurethane. The finished piece will look like that in figure 84.

Figure 84 *The finished inner mold assembly.*

The mold press . . .

On the PVC mold we made we were able to use the drill press to compress the clay and to eject the crucible from the mold. Since the concrete mold weighs close to 50 pounds we don't want to move it around any more than we have to. You can make your own very effective press from angle iron and lumber and attach it to the concrete mold.

Figure 85 *The concrete mold and press.*

The complete set up is shown in the photo figure 85. The individual parts of the press fixture and assembly details are given on the next couple of pages.

First, you will need to make the clamp frame which consists of two pieces of angle iron that are clamped to the mold with 1/2" x 10" carriage bolts as shown in figure 88. The top clamp detail is shown in figure 86 and is made from 2 x 2 x 1/4" angle iron. The bottom clamp detail is shown in figure 87. It is made from 1-1/2" x 1-1/2" x 1/4" angle.

The lever arm in figure 89 is a 24" long 2 x 4 with a 1/2" hole drilled through on center, 2" back from one end. The lever arm is inserted between the pivot posts and held in place with a 1/2" bolt or a piece of threaded rod 4" long. See figure 92.

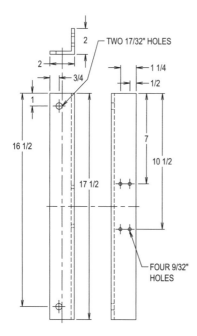

Figure 86 Top clamp detail. Make one from 2" x 2" x 1/4" angle.

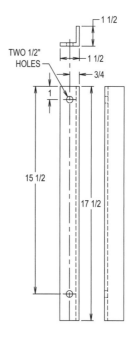

Figure 87 The bottom clamp/leg detail. Make 1 from 1-1/2" x 1-1/2" x 1/4" angle iron.

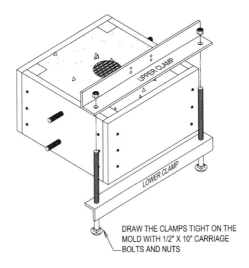

Figure 88 Attaching the clamp frame to the mold using 1/2" x 10" carriage bolts and nuts.

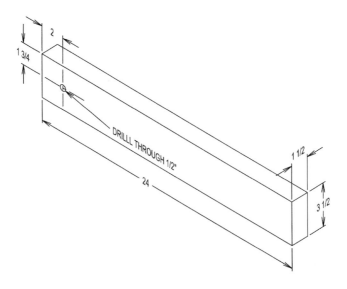

Figure 89 The lever arm. Make one from a 24" long 2 x 4.

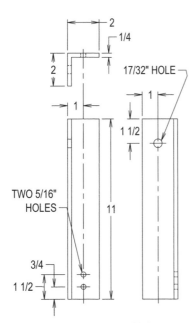

Figure 90 Pivot post detail. Make an opposing pair from 2" x 2" x 1/2" angle iron.

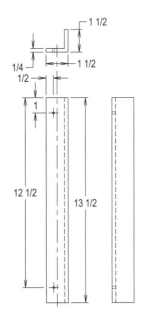

Figure 91 The front leg. Make one from 1-1/2" x 1-1/2" x 1/4" angle.

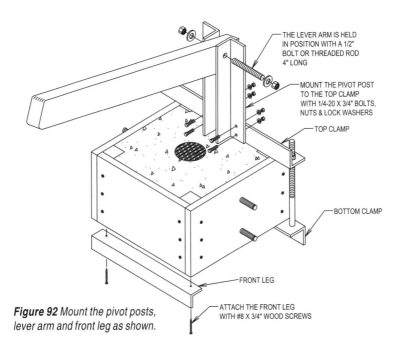

Figure 92 Mount the pivot posts, lever arm and front leg as shown.

Speaking of pivot posts, you will need to make two of them as shown in figure 90 from 2 x 2 x 1/4" angle iron. They are bolted to a clamp frame with 1/4-20 x 3/4" bolts and nuts as shown in figure 92.

Also make the front leg from 1/4" x 1-1/2" x 1-1/2" angle as shown in figure 91. It is mounted to the bottom front edge of the mold as shown in figure 92.

The ram is a 1-1/2" x 1-1/2" square board 8-1/2" long with a 5/16" hole drilled through one end as shown in figure 93.

The brackets for attaching the ram to lever arm are shown in figure 94. Holes are drilled in the brackets as shown. Two are needed.

The brackets are first attached to the ram with a 2" long 1/4" bolt or length of threaded rod. Then center the ram over the mold cavity and allow for a space of 1/4" between the ram and the lever arm. Attach the other end of each bracket to the lever arm with wood screws as shown in figure 95.

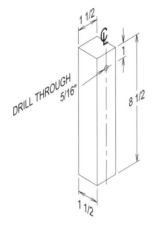

Figure 93 The ram. Make one from a 1-1/2" x 1-1/2" x 8-1/2" board.

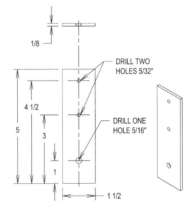

Figure 94 Brackets for mounting the ram to the pivot post.. Make two from 1-1/2" x 1/8" strap iron.

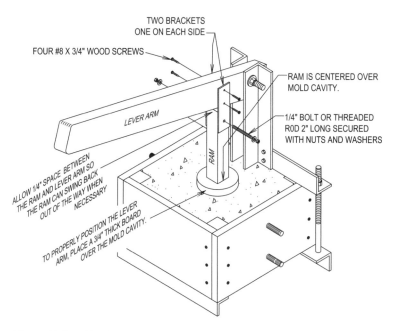

Figure 95 *Attaching the ram to the lever arm. First, attach the brackets to the ram with a 1/4-20 x 2 bolt and nut or threaded rod. Then center the ram over the mold cavity. Ensure a 1/4" space exists between the ram and the lever arm. When positioned, screw the brackets to the lever arm as shown.*

You will need two fixtures for compressing the clay in the mold. One is a flat circular piece of wood turned to a diameter that just fits inside the mold cavity. On my mold, that diameter was just slightly less than 4".

The other fixture for a lack of a better term is referred to as the edge fixture. It is used to enhance the ability to compact the clay at the edge or wall of the crucible.

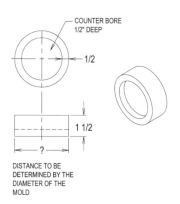

Figure 96 *The edge fixture made from a block of wood.*

51

The drawing in figure 96 will give you an idea of what the fixture should look like. Such a fixture could be turned on the lathe from a piece of wood. Or; I used a PVC DWF flush bushing that only required a slight modification. You might consider this as an option rather than making one from a block of wood. A photo of the modified fitting can be seen in figure 97.

Figure 97 *An edge fixture made from a PVC DWF fllush bushing. Such bushings are available at home supply centers.*

How to use the crucible making machine . . .

The concrete crucible making machine is very easy to use. The photos and step by step instructions on the next few pages will take you through the process.

But first, you will need to mix up a batch of clay. To make this crucible will require 4 pounds of mix. The recipe is in the adjoining column.

<u>Recipe for 4 pounds of clay.</u> . .

24 ounces of fire clay

1 ounce of Potash Feldspar

39 ounces of grog

For mixing instructions, refer back to the information beginning on page 24.

Figure 98 *This is how things will look before you get started. The concrete mold is on the right and the inner form is shown on the left.*

Figure 99 Petroleum jelly is a good release agent. Coating the inner mold form and the inside walls of the mold cavity with it will make the finished crucible much easier to remove from the mold.

Figure 100 Raise the concrete form up on its side and insert the inner mold into the concrete mold cavity as shown.

Figure 101 lower the concrete form back down ensuring the inner form remains in position. Then regular screen door hooks are used to secure the inner mold and prevent it from being pushed out when compressing the clay.

Figure 102 Top view looking down into the mold cavity. Inner form is in position and we are ready to begin ramming in the clay.

Figure 103 Here we are ramming in the clay. I am using a 1/2" x 3/4" pine stick 18" long to ram the clay. One of the most important things in the process is to insure the clay is rammed firmly in the mold. So add the clay in layers a little bit at a time tightly ramming each layer. If when applying pressure to the ram stick the clay feels spongy, then you haven't rammed tight enough. Continue this process until the mold is full.

Figure 104 The edge fixture is placed over the mold cavity. The ram is brought down on the fixture and force is applied to the lever arm. Continue adding clay and repeating this procedure until the edge of the mold is tightly packed.

Figure 105 Add more clay as needed and compress the mold with the round disk fixture. Repeat this as many times as necessary until the mold full and the clay is firmly compacted.

Figure 106 Further compacting the clay in the mold with a rubber mallet.

Figure 107 Rammed full and ready for the next step.

55

Figure 108 Turn the concrete form up on its side. Undo the hooks holding the inner mold in position and give the inner mold a slight twist as shown. Do not remove the mold, just loosen it.

Figure 109 Roll the concrete form back down ensuring that the inner mold remains intact. Place spacers under both legs as shown. Spacers can be wood or metal and no more than 1/2" is necessary. We are getting ready to press the crucible out of the mold and the inner mold must remain intact to support the clay form as it drops.

Figure 110 Place the compression disk on top of the clay form. Apply pressure to the lever arm to eject the crucible from the mold.

Figure 111 Carefully lift the concrete form straight up and high enough to clear the crucible and set it over to one side. The mold weighs about 50 pounds which is fairly heavy. Use proper lifting technique and if necessary get help in lifting it.

Figure 112 The concrete form has been raised and placed to one side exposing the finished crucible.

Figure 113 Place a sheet of metal or board on the bottom of the crucible. Then with the crucible sandwiched as shown turn it over so that it is upright.

Figure 114 Carefully lift the inner mold and set it to one side.

Figure 115 A newly formed clay crucible.

After letting the crucible air dry for a few days, you will be ready to fire it. Refer to pages 29 through 33 for firing instructions.

I have found that a coating of glaze on the crucible is beneficial and will extend its life. Remember, you must first fire the crucible before applying the glaze. Then refire the crucible to set the glaze. Instructions for making and applying the glaze are on page 33.

A source for commercial glaze is.

www.budgetcastingsupply.com

Well, there you have it. You're ready to make your own crucibles. Before your first pour, be sure and review the top ten list of safety rules for all metals on the following page. Above all BE SAFE. Best wishes for success in all of your shop projects.

Figure 116 Use a utility knife to cut a "V" shaped notch into the inside edge of the pouring spout.

Figure 117 Pouring a casting with a crucible produced in the concrete mold. You may not be able to tell from the photo, but this crucible has been glazed.

*Top ten list of safety rules. . .

Each metal has its peculiarities that must be learned as you use them, but all of them deserve a basic respect. These rules are in the interest of safety.

1. Use only sound crucibles. A cracked pot is on the verge of breaking.

2. Use only properly fitting tongs.

3. Don't try to handle a crucible brim full of metal.

4. Preheat metal that is to be added to a pot of molten metal. You can set it on the furnace lid near the vent or hold it over the vent with the tongs. Plunging cold metal into a pot can cause a violent explosion.

5. Use tongs to gently add metal to a pot. Never drop it in.

6. Add only moderate amounts of metal to a pot to avoid chilling the melt.

7. Examine all of your scrap piece by piece. A coffee can of small scrap could contain something dangerous.

8. Make sure there is no trapped liquid in any scrap that is added to a pot of molten metal.

9. Don't cool skimmers, stirring rods or tongs in water. A wet tool in contact with molten metal is very dangerous.

10. Always have ample ingot or pig molds to dispose of all the metal you melt in case a mold fails.

*The top ten list is from the book, "Building A Gas Fired Crucible Furnace" by David J. Gingery ISBN 1-878087-08-8

Final thoughts . . .

It is best to let crucibles air dry or cure for extended periods of time before use. If you make them up in advance as I do, you will need a warm dry place to keep them. The old foundry shops would store crucibles on the annealing oven or near the flues of the melting furnaces. It is likely you won't have that advantage, but I have found the attic of my house well suited for curing crucibles. In the summer time temperatures there will get well over 100 degrees.

Remember to preheat your crucible before use. Then add metal gradually. Never cram or force metal into the pot. When you have finished pouring, return the crucible to the furnace immediately and close the lid thus allowing the crucible to cool slowly.

**Typical sizes for clay graphite crucibles. . .*

	OD*	Ht.
#0000	2-5/8" x	3-1/16 "
#1	3-5/16" x	3-13/16"
#2	3-7/8" x	4-1/2"
#3	4-3/8" x	5-13/16"
#4	4-3/4" x	5-1/2"
#6	5-3/4" x	6-3/4"
#8	5-7/8" x	7-3/16"

*OD measured at the top of the crucible.
** Assuming wall thickness of 5/8".